JUN 2 8 2016

DISCARDED BY
MEMPHIS PUBLIC LIBRARY

United States Regions

Mountain Region

Anastasia Suen

rourkeeducationalmedia.com

Scan for Related Titles
and Teacher Resources

Before Reading:

Building Academic Vocabulary and Background Knowledge

Before reading a book, it is important to tap into what your child or students already know about the topic. This will help them develop their vocabulary, increase their reading comprehension, and make connections across the curriculum.

1. Look at the cover of the book. What will this book be about?
2. What do you already know about the topic?
3. Let's study the Table of Contents. What will you learn about in the book's chapters?
4. What would you like to learn about this topic? Do you think you might learn about it from this book? Why or why not?
5. Use a reading journal to write about your knowledge of this topic. Record what you already know about the topic and what you hope to learn about the topic.
6. Read the book.
7. In your reading journal, record what you learned about the topic and your response to the book.
8. After reading the book complete the activities below.

Content Area Vocabulary
Read the list. What do these words mean?

ancient
basin
continent
divide
geography
glaciers
government
playa
political
range
ridge
volcanoes

After Reading:

Comprehension and Extension Activity

After reading the book, work on the following questions with your child or students in order to check their level of reading comprehension and content mastery.

1. What are some obstacles that settlers encountered traveling through the mountain ranges? (Asking questions)
2. What resources are sought after in the Rocky Mountains? (Summarize)
3. In what ways is the Great Basin Desert different from other deserts? (Asking questions)
4. Why can't fish live in the Great Salt Lake? (Infer)
5. Why are the Rocky Mountains a popular vacation spot? (Asking questions)

Extension Activity

How were the Rocky Mountains formed? Using graham crackers you will be able to explain how mountains are formed. You will need a shallow dish, two graham crackers, and water. Add a very thin layer of water to the dish. Place the two graham crackers on top of the water allowing them to absorb some water but not become soggy. Before too much water is absorbed, push the graham crackers together. What do the graham crackers represent? What is happening when the graham crackers collide? How does this relate to how mountains form?

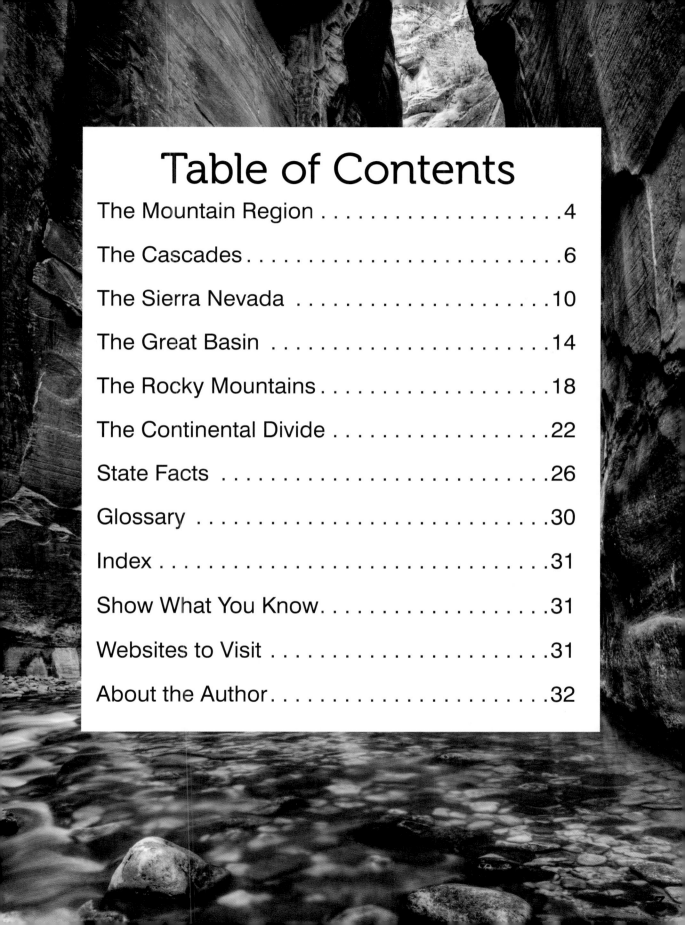

Table of Contents

The Mountain Region

Geography is useful to break land areas up into regions with common features. The Mountain region in the West has mountains on the east side and mountains on the west side. The land in the middle is desert.

*The lines drawn on this map are **political** lines. They show the borders for each state's government.*

The Half Dome, located in Yosemite National Park, is a challenge and adventure for hikers.

The region falls between the West Coast, Midwest, and Southwest regions. States that fall in the Mountain region are Washington, Oregon, California, Nevada, Idaho, Utah, Montana, Wyoming, and Colorado.

The Cascades

The Cascades are a chain of mountains in the Northwest. These **ancient** mountains are **volcanoes**.

The Mount St. Helens volcano erupted in 1980. The blast flattened trees and homes for 230 square miles (370 square kilometers). The plume of ash and steam was more than 12 miles (19.3 kilometers) high.

In the United States, the Cascades begin with Mount Baker in Washington State. This mountain range ends at Lassen Peak in Northern California.

The Mount St. Helens eruption was the most destructive in U.S. history.

When you visit the Cascades, you will find miles of evergreen forest. Some places are so cold that they have **glaciers**. These giant sheets of ice form between the mountains.

Crater Lake in Oregon is 1,943 feet (592 kilometers) deep. That makes it the deepest lake in the United States. It is also the ninth deepest lake in the world.

The Chinook Indian tribes fished in the Pacific Ocean and the Columbia River. They made different canoes for traveling in the river and traveling in the ocean.

People have been living in the Cascades for thousands of years. Native people crossed the mountains to trade with each other.

Europeans started coming in the late 1700s. They came for what they could find on the land. Trappers sold the furs they caught to buyers all over the world. Miners came to look for gold and silver. Loggers came to cut down the trees for wood and paper.

In 1841, American settlers started coming to the Cascades. They walked 2,000 miles (3,218 kilometers) from Missouri to Oregon. They called their path the Oregon Trail.

In 1848, Congress created the Oregon Territory. This large area is now five different states.

The Sierra Nevada

The Sierra Nevada is another mountain **range**. It is south of the Cascades. There are volcanoes here too. But these volcanoes have not been active for 10 million years. Long ago there were also glaciers here. Glaciers carved Yosemite Valley out of the granite there. Hundreds of thousands of people visit Yosemite National Park each month.

Most of the Sierra Nevada is in California. Only a small part in the North, near Lake Tahoe, is in Nevada.

Yosemite Valley is home to deep valleys, giant sequoias, and grand

Donner Pass is named after a group of settlers. Many people in the Donner party died here when they tried to cross during the winter.

It's hard to cross the mountains. In the Sierras, the best place is Donner Pass. Just don't try it in the winter. It snows 34 feet (10.3 meters) a year!

You can see the history of travel at this pass near Lake Tahoe. The Washoe people walked across the pass. The pass became an important route to the West. The first railroad across the country went through Donner Pass. It was also part of the first highway across the country. Even the first airline route across the country followed Donner Pass.

In the mid-1800s, gold was discovered in the western foothills of the Sierras. Many people flocked to the region to seek their fortunes. When gold was no longer abundant, people logged the forests, including the many giant sequoias.

Today, much of the Sierra Nevada is protected. Logging the giant sequoias is no longer allowed. People in the region go hiking and camping in the beautiful mountains.

The Great Basin

The Great **Basin** Desert is the largest desert in the United States. High above sea level, this is a cold desert. Only one inch (2.54 centimeters) of rain or snow falls each month.

The Great Basin Desert covers 200,000 square miles (322,000 square kilometers).

The Great Basin isn't just one basin. There are many basins in this area. All of the water in a basin stays there. It sinks into the ground or flows into lakes. The Great Salt Lake is the largest lake in the area. Only algae, brine shrimp, and brine flies live in the lake, which is too salty for fish. When a small lake like this dries up, only the salt is left. The lake has changed into a **playa**.

Water that falls in the Great Basin drains into the Great Salt Lake, Bear Lake, Utah Lake, and other basins.

The Great Salt Lake is the largest salt lake in the western hemisphere.

Long ago, the Fremont people lived in villages. Their houses were made of adobe. They grew corn, beans, and squash. Explorers from Europe came to the Great Basin in the 1700s. But they didn't stay. A hundred years later, American settlers came. They started farms and ranches. Miners came, too. They looked for gold, silver, and copper. Small mining towns started.

People made their homes with what they could find. In a place with very little rain, the homes were made with adobe bricks. These bricks of straw and clay were dried in the sun.

Mining and cattle ranching remain two big industries for the area today. Ranchers herd cattle up and down the basin to graze on hay and other grasses. Gold is still mined, but other minerals such as copper, gypsum, and lithium are mined as well.

The Rocky Mountains

The Rocky Mountains are almost 3,000 miles (4,828 kilometers) long. They stretch across the entire **continent**. They begin in Canada and end in Mexico. There are more than 100 mountain ranges in this mountain chain.

Idaho, Montana, Wyoming, Utah, and Colorado are known as the Rocky Mountain states.

Yellowstone National Park is a national park known for its wildlife and geysers. The geysers spout hot water high into the air. The park was created when a volcano exploded there about 640,000 years ago. The park formed in the crater left by the explosion.

The Rocky Mountains are highlands. The high elevation makes the winters very cold. There is a lot of snow, and blizzards are common.

People have lived in the Rocky Mountains for ten thousand years. The Ute tribe followed the herds. They moved where the animals were grazing.

Trappers and miners both came to the Rockies. Today coal is mined there.

The snowshoe hare grows white fur in the winter. The rest of the year it has brown fur.

Coal is mined in the Powder River Basin in Wyoming. This coal is used to generate electricity.

When you visit the Rockies you can ski in the winter and hike in the summer.

The Rockies are a favorite vacation spot. The higher you go in the mountains, the thinner the air is. It takes time to get used to breathing less oxygen. Be sure to drink a lot of water. Don't try to climb too high too fast.

The Continental Divide

The land at the top of a mountain is called a **ridge**. In the Rocky Mountains, the water flows in two directions. On one side of the ridge it flows east. On the other side, it flows west. This type of ridge is called a **divide**.

The Continental Divide in the Rockies divides the waters in our continent.

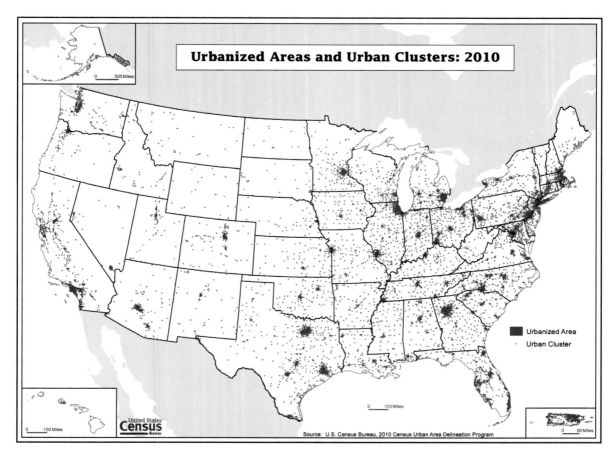

Many people live in urban areas (purple) and urban clusters (green). Few people live in rural (white) areas.

Every ten years, the **government** counts all of the people in the country. This is called a census. The numbers can be used in many ways. One way is to look at who lives where.

Some people live in urban areas or cities with lots of people. Others live in rural areas and small towns. They may live on farms or ranches. Most of the Mountain West is rural.

Horehound Candy Recipe

Settlers made this candy to help coughs and colds

Ingredients:

1 ounce dried **horehound** herb

1 3/4 pounds brown sugar

4 tablespoons corn syrup

1 1/2 cups water

Directions:

Cook horehound and water slowly for 30 minutes.

Remove the horehound.

Add brown sugar and syrup.

Cook the mixture to 300°F. (Use a candy thermometer to test it.)

Pour into a well-greased pan. Mark into squares as the candy

begins to harden.

The people in the Mountain region are strong and independent. Many of them enjoy the outdoors and love to take advantage of the great sights that their region has to offer. Hiking, skiing, and mountain climbing are all popular activities. The Mountain region is just one of the great parts of our United States.

State Facts Sheet

Washington

Motto: Bye and Bye.

Nickname: The Evergreen State

Capital: Olympia

Known for: Apples, Mt. St. Helens, the Space Needle

Fun Fact: The world's largest building, a Boeing assembly plant, is located in Everett, Washington.

Oregon

Motto: She Flies With Her Own Wings.

Nickname: The Beaver State

Capital: Salem

Known for: Crater Lake, Tillamook Cheese, Dunes

Fun Fact: Oregon has more ghost towns than any other state.

California

Motto: Eureka...I Have Found It!
Nickname: The Golden State
Capital: Sacramento
Known for: Hollywood, Beaches, Wine Country, Golden Gate Bridge
Fun Fact: In California, Death Valley is the hottest, driest place in the U.S. It reaches 115° Fahrenheit (46° Celsius) in summer.

Nevada

Motto: All For Our Country Battle Born.
Nickname: The Silver State
Capital: Carson City
Known for: Desert, Mountains, Mining, Gold, Las Vegas, Gambling
Fun Fact: Nevada is the largest gold-producing state in the nation.

Idaho

Motto: Let It Be Perpetual.
Nickname: The Gem State
Capital: Boise
Known for: Elk Herds, Potatoes
Fun Fact: The deepest gorge in the U.S. is in Idaho's Hell's Canyon.

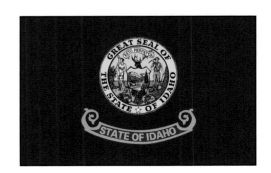

Montana

Motto: Gold and Silver.

Nickname: The Treasure State

Capital: Helena

Known for: Wildlife, Glacier Park, Yellowstone Park

Fun Fact: An average square mile in Montana has 1.4 elk, 1.4 pronghorn antelope, and 3.3 deer.

Wyoming

Motto: Equal Rights.

Nickname: The Equality or Cowboy State

Capital: Cheyenne

Known for: Yellowstone Park, Old Faithful Geyser, Jackson Hole, Buffalo Bill, Coal

Fun Fact: Wyoming was the first state to give women the right to vote.

Colorado

Motto: Nothing Without the Deity.

Nickname: The Centennial State

Capital: Denver

Known for: Skiing, Rocky Mountains, Pike's Peak, Forests, Mining

Fun Fact: The world's largest flattop mountain is in Grand Mesa.

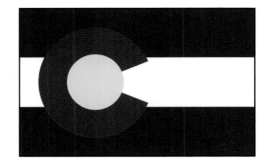

Utah

Motto: Industry.

Nickname: The Beehive State

Capital: Salt Lake City

Known for: Rock Formations, The Great Salt Lake, Skiing

Fun Fact: Utah is named for the Ute tribe, which means, people of the mountains.

Glossary

ancient (AYN-shunt): very old

basin (BAY-suhn): an area of land that drains into a river

continent (KON-tuh-nuhnt): one of seven large land masses of the Earth

divide (duh-VIDE): to split into parts

geography (jee-OG-ruh-fee): the study of the earth

glaciers (GALY-shurz): huge sheets of ice found between mountains

government (GUHV-urn-muhnt): the people who rule a state or country

playa (PLYE-uh): the salty area of land left after a lake dries up

political (pol-IT-uh-kuhl): belonging to the people who run the government

range (RAYNJ): a long chain of mountains

ridge (RIJ): the narrow top of a mountain

volcanoes (vol-KAY-nohz): mountains with vents that let out lava, ash and gas

Index

Show What You Know

1. How have volcanoes and glaciers changed the land in our country?
2. How do we know that people have lived in the Mountain region for more than ten thousand years?
3. Why are some deserts hot while others are cold?
4. Why do animals move from place to place as the seasons change in the mountains?
5. Compare a physical map with the census map. How are geography and population related? How does the land influence where people live?

Websites to Visit

www.nps.gov/yose/

www.nps.gov/grba/

www.nps.gov/yell/

Author

Anastasia Suen saw snow for the first time in the Sierra Nevada Mountains. She has also visited the Cascades and driven across the Great Basin and the Continental Divide in the Rockies. She lives with her family in Plano, Texas.

Meet The Author!
www.meetREMauthors.com

© 2015 Rourke Educational Media

All rights reserved. No part of this book may be reproduced or utilized in any form or by any means, electronic or mechanical including photocopying, recording, or by any information storage and retrieval system without permission in writing from the publisher.

www.rourkeeducationalmedia.com

PHOTO CREDITS: Title page © bjul; page 3 ©liteserv; page 5 © National Park Service, Krystal Hogan; page 6 © Aaron Rutten; page 7 © mkenorton; page 8 © Library of Congress; page 9 © Donna Beeler; page 11 © Everett Collection; page 12 © picturin; page 13 © aslysun; page 14 © GeoBob's Photography; page 15 © Johnny Adolphson; page 16 © Tom Baker, Scott Lathan; page 17 © Terry W Ryder; page 18 © ABDESIGN; page 19 © Edward Fielding; page 20 © Martyne Simard; page 22 © ,areli;oase; page 24 © Louella 938; page 25 © Alxcrs
Edited by: Jill Sherman

Cover design by: Jen Thomas
Interior design by: Rhea Magaro

Library of Congress PCN Data

Mountain Region / Anastasia Suen
(United States Regions)
ISBN 978-1-62717-669-9 (hard cover)
ISBN 978-1-62717-791-7 (soft cover)
ISBN 978-1-62717-908-9 (e-Book)
Library of Congress Control Number: 2014934377

Also Available as:

Printed in the United States of America, North Mankato, Minnesota